Maud Ballington Booth

Branded

A monograph on prison work

Maud Ballington Booth

Branded
A monograph on prison work

ISBN/EAN: 9783744758659

Printed in Europe, USA, Canada, Australia, Japan

Cover: Foto ©ninafisch / pixelio.de

More available books at **www.hansebooks.com**

BRANDED

..A..
Monograph on
Prison Work

BY

MRS. BALLINGTON BOOTH

TORONTO:

WILLIAM BRIGGS

Montreal : C. W. Coates.   Halifax : S. F. Huestis.

1897.

BRANDED.

A DARK night with chilly wind and surging billows, a dangerous coast, a ship in distress, would bring from their happy firesides and homes of comfort a great, anxious crowd. Many eyes would be strained to watch the fight of the human souls in peril; many would wait with bated breath and follow their struggles with the fierce waves with painful suspense. When at last they leaped from the drifting wreck, and life depended upon strength of arm and courage of heart, and they were seen battling shore-

5

ward, buffeted by foaming wave-crests, threatened by chilly depths and increasing exhaustion, — then hearts would almost stop beating and lips would part in an agony of prayer, " God help them ! " I imagine the distance safely covered, the struggling swimmers reaching shore, their weak, benumbed hands stretched out to grasp and hold, with the grip for life, to the seaweed and rocks. You would then look to see every strong arm extended to help them, warm, loving hands grasping theirs firmly, while every muscle was strained to save them from the angry, foaming waves. What a chill of horror, what a thrill of indignation would overwhelm you if you saw the crowd on the beach lean over and deliberately loosen those poor cold hands, and push back into the hungry waters the poor wretches who had made so brave a fight for life. You turn from my picture with a smile and say, " Such a scene would be impossible; men are too human; no one could do so foul a deed of cruelty, or should one even attempt it, scores would defeat his object and rescue his victim ! " I agree with you, — upon an ocean beach in a civilized world, no such fate could await a shipwrecked crew; and yet I can draw an analogy from this picture, and I am prepared to prove that the attitude of the world towards the criminal to-day is such that in his struggle back to honest and right living he is thwarted and cast back into the sea of despair and vice in precisely as cruel and inhuman a way as I have described.

One of the greatest problems of the hour is that which affects the criminals in this, our free America, and it seems to me that one of the first questions to be asked is, " What has made the problem so unsolvable, and where does the responsibility lie ? " With what I have seen and what I have learned I cannot hold the criminal entirely responsible for his seemingly unreachable and irreclaimable position. While the world despises and distrusts him, while it adheres to its old adage, " Once a thief, always a thief ! "

while it closes to him all avenues of escape, the responsibility cannot rest wholly at the door of the criminal. Is it not manifestly wrong to punish a man indefinitely for a crime he has expiated in the eyes of the law, merely because it is possible he may commit another similar offence? Is there anything more calculated to rob him of all hope for his future than a sentiment against him that makes a criminal slink from the prison door on the first day of his release, a very Cain, marked and branded, with the consciousness burned into his very soul that his imprisonment has made him an object of contempt to his fellow men? Is it a wonder that a man distrusts his own power to be good or to make a success of life when he is made to feel that no one else will trust him or believe him capable of good? I speak from an intimate knowledge of prisoners, and I can say emphatically that much of their hopelessness and loss of confidence as to .their ever regaining a place amongst the honest and honorable citizens and wage-earners of the country, springs from the feeling that they are regarded as having fallen from a position which the world feels they can never regain.

I have heard over and over again until my heart has ached the story of how hopefully the " first term " man has stepped forth once more to liberty. He has learned his bitter lesson, has seen his folly, and has looked hopefully to the time when he would at last have a chance to live and work in the free, outside world and make a brave fight to regain what he had lost of the esteem and confidence and friendship of others. Plans and hopes fill his waking and dreaming thoughts, and it is with a glad, joyous heart that he steps forth after the last long wakeful night, once more a free man. The garb of shame, the bolts and bars of convict life, the hated lockstep, the narrow cell, are all behind him, and he says as he turns away, " I will never, never come back ! " Some of those who have seen a little more of life in just these channels

have said to him, " Others have left, saying they would never come back, and yet
they *have* come back ! " but he smiles
pityingly at their weakness, knowing his
resolve is firm, and thus he goes forth
bravely to fight and struggle, fearing not
but that he will succeed.   But alas !   It
is often all in vain !   He has a little
money, a suit of clothes.   If he has a
home there is a shade more hope for him,
but in many cases he is homeless, and
perhaps has no friends in this country ;
or maybe his mother or wife has died
since he left home, or, as in some cases,
his friends have disowned him because of
his disgrace.   " Well, never mind," says
the world, " he must expect *that*, he is

suffering for his sin. Let him go to work and prove that he is in earnest!" That is precisely what he wants to do; but will the people who say this so easily without a thought of all it means, tell us how and where he is to get work? Day after day passes, and he begins tc realize how hard it is. He tramps the streets from early to late; he answers advertisements; he offers his services here, there, and everywhere, until hope begins to wane. His money is going; he is weary and hungry, and he has to face the facts and they are not as he would like them to be. He is willing to work for his board and lodging, but even this he cannot do, — nobody wants him ! The bright hope fades from his sky; sullen despair and hopelessness settle on his soul. Then comes the time when money is gone; he still walks the street looking for work, but his step is lagging and unsteady from faintness, and he has to sleep in the Park at night or walk on and on through the lonely, deserted streets. Hunger is followed by starvation and desperation, and then alas! though not till then, thank God, for he was in earnest, he gives way to the tempter, "You must live; you have at least a right to live. Every human being has, and if no one will help you, if no one cares whether you live honestly or not, what are the odds? You know how you can get money, while by right living you can only starve!" This is the natural argument that goes on in the heart that has become hopeless and despairing, and feels to the full the bitter irony of the situation. Then, he gives up the fight, and not so very long after, perhaps, he stands once more before the bar of Justice. "Second offence — only so long from State prison " —so the history goes, and with hardened heart and embittered soul he joins again the marching thousands to whom the lockstep has become the tread of fate. Those who remember him smile bitterly and gain fresh hopelessness as they pass the word along, "back again," taking it as one more sign of the inevitable doom that falls on those who are once branded with the name "convict." To the man who has had more than the one term, is generally added the constant haunting of ever watchful detectives, who follow him about from place to place, always expecting that he is up to some new game, and who are ever too quick to inform against him should he gain honest employment.

Now, perhaps you say this picture is overdrawn. I answer from a personal knowledge of the histories of many, "It is not," and I feel pretty sure that Wardens, Chaplains, and Keepers within the State prisons would most emphatically endorse what I have said. Of course there are many cases where the man is fortunate enough to find work, but alas !

even then it is often only to have his bright
hopes blighted by the discovery being
made that he was once in State prison,
which means discharge; and in many
cases is added the extra handicap of
a weakened constitution and shattered
nerves. When men have come to me
first from State prison, I have noted the
trembling hand, the nervous hunted look,
the stammering words, and I have said to
myself, " If no hand is stretched out to
help him, how can this man be expected
by the world to take his place in society
again at once and earn his own living?"
I turn away, not to marvel that so many
fall, but rather to wonder how any escape.
I wish some of the good and righteous

members of the community who look
down upon the criminal as a weak degen-
erate who gravitates naturally to crime,
could find themselves for a short time in
his tight place.   Should you tell such a
one that the one-time prisoner often gets
to the place where he must steal or
starve, they say with righteous self-con-
sciousness, " Well, I would rather starve ! "
Would they?   They have not tried it, nor
have they tried what is far worse to bear,
— the watching of dear ones' faces growing whiter and thinner for the need of
food ; the bare room and the dread of
losing even that semblance of home, and
I tell you if they HAD, many of your
honest, righteous men of to-day would be

just where our poor " boys " are, — behind the bars !

I do not want to justify crime. I
loathe it. I do not want to sentimental-
ize over the prisoner. The " boys " in
prison know that I am too practical to
be a sentimentalist; but I do want to
show up bare facts, horrible as they may
seem to be. I maintain that many of
those who fall again make a braver fight
before that fall in trying to regain an
honest position in life, than the honest
and righteous man makes to keep his
clean, good record and his honorable
position. It is far easier to remain in
the right path when you have been
trained to walk therein than it is to re-

gain that path when you have once strayed from it. Of course, there are many and many of them who go from State prison without any thought of struggling for a new life. They gravitate back to their old habits, their old companions, and old acts, but of them I am also forced to say that I do not wonder. Hunt up the life history; take into consideration the evidence which no court of justice would listen to but the great court of high heaven, and then your view of their reckless, lawless lives may change, and you may find for them some pity and sorrow. Perhaps they have never had a chance; never were loved or trained or inspired with good desires. No work of reformation has ever reached them. They do not see the good of working hard to gain a meagre existence, when they can get plenty by skill of hand or plot of brain in an unlawful way. Again, many of these have become so hopeless of any other life being possible to them that they have just settled down to accept the inevitable. These old-time habitual criminals are many of them good at heart, — thieves, burglars, robbers, bank-wreckers, I grant you, and yet they have feelings of large-heartedness and generosity which are sometimes lacking in some law-abiding citizens. When talking of the heathen and little children, are we

not accustomed to say that people are
held responsible for the light they have
and not for the light that has not been
shed on their paths? Have we a right
to judge these men in State prison from
our happy and fortunate standpoint?
When I have come time and time again
in contact with lives to whom had never
come the inspiration of a vitally loving,
practical religion before, I have seen
them grasp at it with hearty earnestness
and follow with a childlike, practical obe-
dience each guidance of the newly
awakened conscience, and I have said
to myself, " I would that those who have
so many chances would appreciate them
as do these who have never had a chance
before ! "

A truly hopeless problem, you may say, after looking upon the picture that I have drawn of the convicts' future, and I agree with you, — an absolutely hopeless one when looked at from the human standpoint. Look down upon the ground and into the shadows, and the night looks black and gloomy indeed; but look up at the sky, and star after star gleams out with rays of hope and comfort. God, who placed these millions upon millions of stars in the faraway heaven, who knows each one and has planned and watched over their course for ages, who Himself created them, is the same God who, in tender love, can watch and bless each wandering soul in the night of sin and despair, and His power can indeed bring hope into this problem. A very bright hope it is to those who have been looking at it long enough to gather all it means for the future.

Time and space do not permit me to go into all the much I might say on this subject, but I will try to outline something of our plans of work, and I would like to add that they are approved and endorsed by the thousands of men who know all about the problem, — not from statistics or from study, but from experience. It is this great hope, this new inspiration that has been born within the prisons, that is to my mind the strongest endorsement of the practical wisdom of our plans of work. "You have struck the right chord," have said the wardens to me. "You have found the solution of at least a part of the problem," have said lawyers and judges and other thoughtful men after we have spoken of the work; but I turn from these voices as of minor importance, and I hear the prolonged shout to cheer us on, and to my heart like a veritable inspiration comes the message from the "boys" themselves. "Go on, we are with you; we believe in this work and will help you prove to the world that the problem can be solved and the criminal can be reclaimed!" I do not give away to the

public the many hundreds of letters that
come to me from prison cells, but in all
of them comes not only a message of
love and appreciation, but a thorough
endorsement of the work, and a growing
hopefulness concerning their own future.

I maintain that work for the men when
they leave State prison would be well-
nigh impossible except in close associa-
tion with work within the walls. These
men are not coming out to knock at
doors or to hunt for the offices of strangers who might be willing to help them.
They are not tramps and professional
beggars, and though they are from State
prison, the large majority of them have
pride and self-respect. They would

rather battle for themselves and struggle and suffer, and I think in many cases would rather go under in the unequal struggle, than become mendicants at the door of charity. They will, however, turn to their friends, — those in whom they have confidence, those to whom they have learned to go for help and advice ; and the very fact that they have a friend is to many of them a safeguard. I feel that our work within the prisons forms the link that will draw them to us, and I believe that it also qualifies us to know just how to help them and teaches us the much we ought to know before we can learn how to deal justly with each case. I must say that where these men trust, where they love, and where they place their confidence, it is with a whole-hearted appreciation and gratitude that is almost pathetic in its intenseness. For the homeless ones we have opened a Home to which they can go in the interim between regaining liberty and finding employment; and for all whom we know to be in earnest we try to find work, thus standing by them as their friends at a time when of all others they are in danger and sore pressed by temptation and trial. Our first Home, which is situated on the outskirts of New York, accommodates forty men, but we have only begun. As funds come to us we shall go on increasing our capacity until hundreds will, I hope, be thus cared for. The place is not stigmatized as a " Prisoners' Home " or an " Ex-Convicts' Shelter," *et cetera.* We chose the name, and after it had been approved in State prison we felt it would do, so " Hope Hall " is the Home to which many a " boy " to-day looks with bright hopes for his home-coming. The place is prettily and tastefully furnished. I did not want it to have anything of the Institution look about it. Its white curtains and white beds will always be appreciated by the one who has been used to the gloom of a prison cell. Its bright library and sitting-room, its pleasant dining-room, and bright flowers all go to banish the memory of the past, and to speak of the gladness of the future.

All the work of the Home is done by the men themselves, — the laundry work, taking care of the horses and cows, the gardening, *et cetera*, as also repairs, painting, and improvement of the premises. We do not have a factory attached to the Home where brooms and shoes and brushes are made. My ideas upon this line may perhaps differ from the ideas of others, but from my knowledge of the men, I think my view of the case is correct. Were we dealing with lazy tramps, I should think it advisable to set them all to some such labor as this; but we are dealing with men who are longing to work ; men who want to go forth as soon as possible and gain a living as other citizens, — they are not men willing to be supported by work *created* for them. They have been making brooms and brushes and shoes for the State for a long time past, and now we want them to feel the necessity and possibility of going forth into the world again just as soon as possible, to gain a living in the way of ordinary citizens. No visitors are allowed to come to this Home. The feelings of the men within it are to be considered as though they were in their own mother's home, shielded from all curious eyes. The "old timer" who has served his

four, five, or even six terms in prison,
and the young fellow who has been up
for his first forgery, and feels bitterly
his first blight and shame, will alike be
welcomed within the walls of Hope Hall.
The "boys" appreciate Hope Hall, because its name does not brand the
place with a haunting shadow of their
past lives. They have left prison; they
have satisfied the law; why should they
be looked upon as ex-convicts; why
should the stigma attach itself to them
still, or to their place of residence? We
call our "boys" who go forth into the
world from this bright home "gradu-
ates," and we are hoping in time that
the cruel word "ex-convict" will be

unused. I very rarely quote from the letters of my friends in prison, but one that has just come to my hand I will give, that the opinion of a man who stands in the position where he ought to know all about the problem, may be read by the readers of this article, who might criticise my views from their outside standpoint.

DEAR MRS. BOOTH, — As you gave all of us " boys " an invitation to write to you, why, I thought that I would do so, and earnestly hope my letter will in no way displease you, and should my letter contain anything which is not just right, please to overlook it.

I want to tell you just how your words

affected me, but honestly speaking, I don't know how to start, but will do the best, I can, so here goes.

Our chaplain told us two weeks ago that you would soon come to speak to us, and I have been waiting and watching for your coming.

When you rose to speak to us, my eyes filled with tears. I could not explain why *then* or *now*, and as you went on and spoke of your work, and spoke of your efforts to aid the poor unfortunates in prison like myself, why, two little streams started down my cheeks; I could not keep them back, try as I would, and if any one would have told me that I could be moved so, why, I would have thought they were crazy. Oh, my dear friend, I can speak from my own *personal* experience, and tell how hard it is for a man leaving prison to do what is right. No doubt you think you know pretty nearly how a man feels, but no one who has not experienced it personally can fully realize the struggle. I was brought up by kind parents, who tried all in their power to make a man of me. When quite young I became a slave to gambling, and was soon behind bars. I "graduated" from one of the "colleges" you visit on the Hudson, and with a strong desire to do what was right and to earn an honest and respectable living. I did try, and

was for a time successful. While working, a "gentleman," just like some of
those you spoke of having trouble with
in "Switzerland," came to the place
where I was working, and told my employer that I was an ex-convict, and was
perhaps planning to rob his place. I
was discharged, my employer telling me
work was slack, which I knew to be a
lie, and shortly after I found out the
reason for my discharge and grew dis-
couraged. A short time found me back
with my old companions, the most reckless of them all, stopping at nothing,
and the end came by my being sent
here. Should you show my letter to
some of the police officials of New

York, no doubt they would smile and say, " Why, Mrs. Booth, that is a most dangerous man ! He is up to some game; be careful of him; he wants to impose upon you in some way." But such is not the case, and *you*, by your *kind words*, can do more to aid *me* and many another man to do what is right than all the police officers in this world. They have put me right where I am to-day by not letting me do what was right. As you spoke of the mother's love, my thoughts went out to my own dear mother, and the last time I saw her in her little cottage home on the outskirts of New York city. I can even now fancy I see her standing in the cottage door, her hand upon my shoulder, telling me to be a good man, and I saying, " I will, mother ! " but the very next day I was committing a crime ; but the poor old mother has died but a few months ago, and all I have to treasure is her memory.

I tell you sincerely it is, oh ! so hard to do what is right when a man once becomes what is known to the police as a " crook." No one will trust him ; the police hound him and want him to give them information regarding others, and no man who has the least spark of manhood left will do that and be the means of others being sent to prison ; and if he refuses to comply with their request they

will soon send him to prison, be he inno-
cent or guilty.

In speaking of "Hope Hall" I thought
what a nice place it must be! Often
when speaking with my companions *in*
prison and *out*, how often have I heard
many of them (and I know a great many
of them, I assure you) speak of the so-
called Homes for discharged prisoners;
how they would speak of them and how
when a man would enter them he would
be looked upon by visitors of the "Home"
as a "freak." But what a difference in
Hope Hall! Oh, what can I say to let
you know just how I feel towards you!
Never during my experience have I heard
of such a work as you are engaged in,

and there are some noble and manly young fellows in prison whom I know your kind words will win. My own future seems to look brighter than it has for a number of years. A kind and Christian officer in this prison has taken an interest in me, and means to give me an opportunity to reclaim myself, and I will try hard to do so. I know it will be a hard battle, but I mean to try hard to win, as I told this dear friend this evening whilst talking with him. He earnestly· desires me to become a Christian like himself, but I tell him honestly I cannot. But I guess he means to try hard to do so. I would like to give you his name but don't like to, but I am going to ask him to write to you himself. He is always ready with the kind word with us " boys," as you term us ; always ready to comfort the needy, and it is something unusual amongst the keepers, I assure you. If he don't write to you, I will tell you his name so that you can write and thank him for his kindness to one of your "boys." I am a New York boy, and I want to be called one of your "boys."

Could you but know what pleasure your visit gave us "boys" I am sure your work would often call you here. Why, the "boys" are going wild over you here I Could you but hear some of their remarks I am sure it would please you. A man sat next to me in church who is one of the most noted criminals in the world, and *you made him cry*. He looked at me and laughed as he saw the tears in my eyes, but a few moments after I looked at him and one great big tear was just dropping into his mouth, which was wide open as he gazed at you.

What more can I say to you ? I told my Christian friend I wanted to write to you and he said, " Very well, do so ! " But wait till he sees my letter ! Three pages, and we are only allowed to write one ! I should have said sheets, but excuse the mistake. All that I see any way as I am writing this is a slight figure in blue, pleading, oh, so earnestly ! It was a sight I shall never forget, and has done me a great deal of good, I assure you.

I would be pleased to receive the Gazette if you have any to spare. I would send the money, but I am "dead broke." My dear friend, I do hope your noble work will be crowned with success. A man who could and would try to impose on you in any way would indeed be a loafer and devoid of all manhood, and I do earnestly hope no one will ever be so mean.

I write this letter and try to speak plainly and honestly, and hope it may give you a little pleasure to know that there was one who most heartily appreciated your kind words, and knew from experience that you spoke words of truth.

I will close my rambling letter by hoping to hear you speak to us again ere long, as we all want to see you.

May God bless and protect *you* and yours from all want and sickness, and may I some day in the future grasp your hand and thank you for your efforts to save me and others. This is the earnest prayer of

Your humble servant,

———

Hundreds of prisoners to-day are looking to their home-coming with joyful expectation, whereas they used to look at it with gloomy foreboding. Had I the money I could open other larger Homes at once, and oh, how I long to rent and furnish them when I think of the many who are coming to us ; but so far we have had to be patient and wait until the public sympathy is touched that will place the means within our hands.

On one score I have no doubt, — the men *will* come to us, and already so strong a link has been forged that without the slightest hesitancy their first thought will be on leaving State prison to come straight to our offices. They have learned to know us in the prisons, and through their correspondence we have come to know them as individuals, learning not only the name and cell number, but much about the past. I feel most strongly that this work must be the *personal* work of friend to friend, or else the most needy and most sensitive would go forth alone carrying their own burden rather than share their hearts' cares with strangers who might not understand.

Of course one of the questions that will be the most difficult for us to solve will be the finding of work for our friends when they have proved themselves at Hope Hall as thoroughly reliable and in earnest. All I can do in this direction is to appeal again and again to Christian gentlemen who are employers of labor, begging them to help me by giving our "boys" a chance. Every profession, trade, and occupation will be represented

by those who come out from the State
prisons : the common laborer, the skilled
mechanic, the accountant, the clerk, the
man of education, gifts, and talents, which
make a position almost more difficult for
him to find than were he accustomed to
the common drudgery. Yet I think I
can say from my personal knowledge that
each and all of them will be ready and
willing to take any position that they can
possibly fill, glad even at small wages to
get the chance to put their foot on the
first round of the ladder that will mean to
them an upward rise. Are these men
worthy of help? If you could see their
manful struggles, if you could know as I
do how sincere is their penitence and

how they long to atone for the past, you would indeed feel them worthy of a strong hand of help and sympathy. May I, through these pages, appeal to the sympathy of Christian fathers and mothers whose own sons are guarded, to sympathize with these boys who are somebody's sons and to whom the great loving father heart of God goes out in yearning? We need money; we need the co-operation of those who could help us in finding work for these men; we need clothing for them; we need all the sympathy and help that can be given them, for this is a problem which cannot be solved by one or two, but which can only be lessened as each sympathetic heart spreads an influence among the unsympathetic which will break down the barriers of prejudice and open up avenues of escape to those who have so long been doomed.

Our work is but young, but in a few years we will prove by living facts, whatever has been said to the contrary, that the criminal can be reclaimed and the one-time convict can be redeemed.

www.ingramcontent.com/pod-product-compliance
Lightning Source LLC
Chambersburg PA
CBHW021430090426
42739CB00009B/1425